Co

Introduction

Everybody has a story.

Your story includes the things you have done, the places you have lived your life, the experiences which have made you who you are, the people who have been most important to you.

Your story is not yours alone, but is also part of lots of other stories – the story of your family, your group of friends, your town or village, your church, even your country.

God has a story too. This is the story of God's loving and creative engagement with the world, which finds its high point in the life, death, resurrection and ascension of Jesus. From one perspective, to be a Christian is to be someone who lives their story in the light of God's story.

Story is an important concept in these Lent reflections. So is witness, which for our purposes is the joyful call to each of us to share our own story of God. So too is evangelism, which is the particular ability God gives to some of us to be able to tell the story of God in a way that stirs faith in those who might not call themselves Christians. All of this will become clearer over the next few weeks.

You have a story to tell, and so do I. Your story is unique, and it is powerful, because it authentic, because it is yours, because it is God's. So let's dive in.

How to Use these Reflections

Each day, Monday to Saturday, try to find 8 to 10 minutes. Read the short Bible passage, perhaps more than once. Sometimes the reflections will encourage you to read a longer passage of the Bible if you have time, to get the full context. Then read the reflection and have a think about what is said. Finally, say your own prayers, using the brief prayer which is given at the end of each day's reflection.

At the start of each week, there is a brief introduction to set the scene for the whole week, with an action for the week. Don't neglect the action! That's how all of this becomes real.

If you would like to dig a bit deeper, there are also resources for small groups, available via: **churchofengland.org/livelent**.

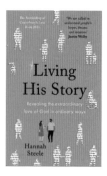

I would also encourage you to consider reading the Archbishop of Canterbury's Lent book for 2021, *Living His Story* by Hannah Steele, on which these reflections are based.

Church House Publishing and I would like to express warmest thanks to Hannah and to SPCK Publishing for allowing me to develop these reflections and to include short extracts from the book in several of them.

Stephen Hance
The Revd Dr Stephen Hance is Evangelism and Discipleship Lead for the Church of England.

The Greatest Story of all Time

This is not a Lent course. Or rather, it's not a plan to take on something difficult as a Lenten discipline, like giving up chocolate or alcohol, something we thankfully lay down on Easter Sunday. Rather, it's an invitation, to find ourselves in the greatest story ever told, and then to invite others into that story with us.

ACTION

This week, take time to reflect on how your own story of faith began. How did God become real to you? You might like to get a journal or notebook and write this down.

Beautiful Feet

READING Romans 10.13-16

"Everyone who calls on the name of the Lord shall be saved." But how are they to call on one in whom they have not believed? And how are they to believe in one of whom they have never heard? And how are they to hear without someone to proclaim him? And how are they to proclaim him unless they are sent? As it is written, "How beautiful are the feet of those who bring good news!"

Not many of us think about our feet as our loveliest feature. Leaders of local churches that include footwashing in their Maundy Thursday services know how difficult it can be to find volunteers. Those who do agree to have their feet washed have probably already given their feet a pretty good wash before they came out!

Yet Paul, quoting Isaiah, says that feet can be beautiful because of the news they bring. If you have ever waited for someone to come and tell you that the baby has been born safely, or the test result has come back clear, or that you got the job you longed for, you probably have a sense of what he means.

Today we begin a journey of discovery, a journey which takes us deep into good news for ourselves and those around us. Our prayer is that by the end of the journey we too might have "beautiful feet"!

PRAYER

Thank you, God, for the people who have brought good news to me, especially those who helped me to understand the good news of your love. Please bless them today.
Amen.

God's Story

READING John 20.1-18

Mary Magdalene went and announced to the disciples, "I have seen the Lord"; and she told them that he had said these things to her. (verse 18)

Everybody loves a story.

We remember the stories we were told as children by those who cared for us with great affection.

We watch films to be gripped by a story. And we find ourselves turning the light off to go to sleep later than we meant to because we were so engrossed in our bedtime reading. "Just one more chapter!"

The Gospel is not primarily a set of doctrinal propositions or metaphysical beliefs, but a story. It's the story of God and God's engagement with the world. It reaches its climax in the life of Jesus. And the story of Jesus hangs on this extraordinary plot twist, that the man who had died was alive again.

Mary Magdalene was the first to experience this. And her immediate response? To share the story with others. "I have seen the Lord!"

PRAYER

Lord Jesus, I may not have 'seen' you, but I have experienced something of you in prayer, worship, the Bible, the Eucharist, other people. Thank you for those moments. Amen.

Living God's Story

READING Matthew 4.18-20 (NLT)

> One day as Jesus was walking along the shore of the Sea of Galilee, he saw two brothers—Simon, also called Peter, and Andrew—throwing a net into the water, for they fished for a living. Jesus called out to them, "Come, follow me, and I will show you how to fish for people!" And they left their nets at once and followed him.

Stories tell us who we are. They tell us where we belong. And they help us to decide who we want to be.

When Jesus calls people, he doesn't call them to an interpretation of the religious law, but into a story. The story into which

Jesus invites us is the story of God's loving engagement with the world. It's the story which begins with God's creation, continues through human wanderings towards and away from God, and reaches its dramatic peak in the coming of Jesus, the Word made flesh. The key word in Jesus' invitation is "follow." Walk in my footsteps, Jesus says, and make my story your story.

The invitation to Christian faith is always an invitation into the story of God, to make God's story our own, and to live out of that story. And here, right at the beginning, Jesus makes clear that accepting this invitation will entail inviting others in as well. "I will show you how to fish for people."

PRAYER

Lord Jesus, thank you for the story of God into which you invite each of us. Help us to understand that story more fully this Lent, and to live it out each day. Amen.

Come
and See

READING John 1.45-47

> Philip found Nathanael and said to him, "We have found him about whom Moses in the law and also the prophets wrote, Jesus son of Joseph from Nazareth." Nathanael said to him, "Can anything good come out of Nazareth?" Philip said to him, "Come and see." When Jesus saw Nathanael coming toward him, he said of him, "Here is truly an Israelite in whom there is no deceit!"

Yesterday we saw how accepting Jesus' invitation into his story always entails inviting others into that story as well. Today we see this in action. Frequently in the Gospels we see ordinary people drawn to Jesus.

Tax collectors and beggars by the roadside find themselves irresistibly pulled towards him. They find themselves welcomed and loved when others had rejected them.

Hannah Steele, in *Living His Story* says: "This kind of invitation can happen anywhere – on a bus or a plane, by the water fountain at work, outside the school gates, by the bedside of a sick friend or to the child on your knee during a bedtime story. And it can happen in so many different ways; through acts of love, through the creative arts, through sharing our experience with others, through pointing to the hidden echoes of the story of Jesus in our world today, through prayer and through healing." All of these can be means to extend that invitation to others: come and see!

PRAYER

Gracious God, your Son Jesus drew all kinds of people to himself, and so to you. Help me to reflect your love so that others may see something of you in me. Amen.

Catching Up with God

Mission is finding out what God is doing, and joining in. This quote, which is often attributed to Archbishop Rowan Williams, reminds us that whenever we think about mission, evangelism, or witnessing to our faith, God is already ahead of us. God is a missionary God, always reaching out in love to the whole creation. Jesus talked about this in stories.

ACTION

This week, take time to read one of the synoptic Gospels (Matthew, Mark or Luke) and reflect on the love that Jesus shows there. You might like to use a journal or notebook to record your observations.

Jesus the Storyteller

READING **Matthew 13.34-35** (NIV)

> Jesus spoke all these things to the crowd in parables; he did not say anything to them without using a parable. So was fulfilled what was spoken through the prophet:
> "I will open my mouth in parables, I will utter things hidden since the creation of the world."

Jesus was a master storyteller. In the synoptic Gospels he is recorded as telling 35 stories, called 'parables'. Many of these – the Good Samaritan, the Prodigal Son - are still well known by many people who otherwise have little knowledge of Christianity. But why did Jesus choose to communicate through parables? Perhaps because the Christian message is not so much a series of propositions to receive in the mind, important though that is, but a new story to be engaged in the imagination.

As Hannah Steele writes in *Living His Story*: "If evangelism is first and foremost an invitation to enter into God's story then the parables can help us picture what it means to enter into and receive this new kingdom. Parables can provide us with a precious window into this alternative way of being in the world, revealing the extraordinary through the ordinary."

We will look at some of these parables this week.

PRAYER

Dear Jesus, thank you for the parables which open up our imaginations to the wonders of your kingdom. Please help me to live out your kingdom story today.
Amen.

The Banquet

"A man prepared a great feast and sent out many invitations. When the banquet was ready, he sent his servant to tell the guests, 'Come, the banquet is ready.' But they all began making excuses... The servant returned and told his master what they had said. His master was furious and said, 'Go quickly into the streets and alleys of the town and invite the poor, the crippled, the blind, and the lame.' After the servant had done this, he reported, 'There is still room for more.' So his master said, 'Go out into the country lanes and behind the hedges and urge anyone you find to come, so that the house will be full.'" (verses 16-18, 21-23)

In this parable a wealthy man has planned a wonderful party and invited all the great and the good of that area. But in the event, all the important invited guests have other things to do. So the host flings wide the doors, sending out a messenger to invite literally everybody, whoever they might be.

We get a picture of God who is not content to include just the powerful or wealthy or even religious people, but who flings open the doors of the heavenly party and sends out to invite everyone in, whoever they may be and wherever they may come from. But don't forget the vital role of the messenger.

Without him going into the streets and giving the message that the banquet is here and the doors are open wide, nobody would have known to come. This sharing of God's invitation is what the Church calls "evangelism."

PRAYER

Loving God, thank you that you invite everyone into your great feast. Please help all those whom you invite to hear your invitation and receive it with joy. Amen.

The Lost Sheep

READING Luke 15.3-7 (NLT)

Jesus told this story: "If a man has a hundred sheep and one of them gets lost, what will he do? Won't he leave the ninety-nine others in the wilderness and go to search for the one that is lost until he finds it? And when he has found it, he will joyfully carry it home on his shoulders. When he arrives, he will call together his friends and neighbours, saying, 'Rejoice with me because I have found my lost sheep.' In the same way, there is more joy in heaven over one lost sinner who repents and returns to God than over ninety-nine others who are righteous and haven't strayed away!"

21

Have you ever lost something? The loss of something apparently quite minor can have a major impact. Your car key is a small thing, but if you lose it a much bigger thing – your car – will not work. Your wallet is a small thing, but if you lose it you may also lose access to your bank account, which is a much bigger thing (or maybe not!) Less dramatically, if you have a complete set of books or records by an artist you love, and one goes missing, somehow it can spoil the whole collection.

This is the first of three parables that Jesus told about things that are lost, all recorded in Luke 15. These stories say something that was very important to Jesus, and Luke doesn't want us to miss it.

PRAYER

Lord, I bring before you something I feel I have lost in my life: whether that is a relationship, a possession, or a dream of how my life would go. Be close to me in that place of loss. Amen.

The Lost Coin

READING Luke 15.8-10 (NLT)

Jesus said, "Or suppose a woman has ten silver coins and loses one. Won't she light a lamp and sweep the entire house and search carefully until she finds it? And when she finds it, she will call in her friends and neighbours and say, 'Rejoice with me because I have found my lost coin.' In the same way, there is joy in the presence of God's angels when even one sinner repents."

The three parables that Jesus tells in Luke 15 are not just about lost things. In fact, only today's reading falls into that category. Another is about a lost sheep, a living creature. Those of us who have treasured pets know how deeply another creature can make its way into a human heart. Yet another is about a lost son.

People can be lost too. A person can be "lost" through a set of broken relationships, through addiction, through some kinds of mental illness. Of course, "lostness" in this case doesn't necessarily mean the person is literally missing. But they may feel that they are lost from others, from the path they were on, from God, even from themselves.

In all these parables, we see a glimpse of God who is always seeking those who are lost. And we are told that when they are found again, there is great rejoicing in heaven.

PRAYER

Loving God, I pray for all who are lost in some way. I ask that you would find them and bring them back to yourself with great rejoicing. Amen.

The Lost Son

READING Luke 15.11-32 (NLT)

"So [the son] returned home to his father. And while he was still a long way off, his father saw him coming. Filled with love and compassion, he ran to his son, embraced him, and kissed him. His son said to him, 'Father, I have sinned against both heaven and you, and I am no longer worthy of being called your son.'

"But his father said to the servants, 'Quick! Bring the finest robe in the house and put it on him. Get a ring for his finger and sandals for his feet. And kill the calf we have been fattening. We must celebrate with a feast, for this son of mine was dead and has now returned to life. He was lost, but now he is found.' " (verses 20-24)

A lost sheep. A lost coin. And now a lost son. Henri Nouwen writes movingly about his first encounter with Rembrandt's painting *The Return of the Prodigal Son* in a book subtitled 'A Story of Homecoming'. Nouwen was at a moment of his life when he felt bone-tired and alone. As he saw a reproduction of this painting, a poster pinned to a door, what spoke to him was its tenderness. The son has returned, filthy, broken, without any of the wealth the father had given him. Yet there is no lecture from the father, no reluctance to receive and embrace the son. There is just tenderness, acceptance, and love.

When we come to God as our loving parent and friend we may be aware of our own poverty and emptiness. Yet God receives us with love, with open arms, with tenderness.

We are welcomed home.

PRAYER

Loving God, thank you that you lookefor us and that you find us and you welcome us into your family. Thank you that you receive us with open arms. Amen.

Compelled by Love

READING **2 Corinthians 5.14-15** (NIV)

For Christ's love compels us, because we are convinced that one died for all, and therefore all died. And he died for all, that those who live should no longer live for themselves but for him who died for them and was raised again.

St Paul makes the point that if we have truly understood the love of Christ for us, then we will feel compelled to share that love with others, in word and deed.

Pope Francis, in *Evangelii Gaudium* (The Joy of the Gospel), writes: "The primary reason for evangelizing is the love of Jesus which we have received, the experience of salvation which urges us to ever greater love of him... If we do not feel an intense desire to share this love, we need to pray insistently that he will once more touch our hearts... What then happens is that 'we speak of what we have seen and heard' (1 John 1:3). The best incentive for sharing the Gospel comes from contemplating it with love, lingering over its pages and reading it with the heart."

Evangelism at its simplest is opening ourselves to the love of Christ to such an extent that this love cannot help but overflow and touch those around us.

PRAYER

Loving Lord, please fill me with your love to such an extent that it overflows from me and touches other people, drawing them to you. Amen.

Stories of Transformation

When Jesus met people, they rarely remained the same. Broken people were made whole, broken relationships were restored, the marginalised found out that God cared for them. Our faith stories are stories of how God has changed us for the better. These stories of life change are powerful.

ACTION

This week, take time to think about how God has changed you. Have there been particular moments when you have known God has been at work in your life? Collect your thoughts in your notebook or journal.

Go Home and Tell

READING Mark 5.1-20

> As Jesus was getting into the boat, the man who had been demon possessed begged to go with him. But Jesus said, "No, go home to your family, and tell them everything the Lord has done for you and how merciful he has been." So the man started off to visit the Ten Towns of that region and began to proclaim the great things Jesus had done for him; and everyone was amazed at what he told them. (verses 18-20)

This is one of the most dramatic stories of a person being changed by Jesus that we have. A man unable to function in society, living wild outside the town, harming himself, is transformed into his right mind, apparently in an instant. No wonder people rushed out to see what had happened.

And no wonder that the man wanted to be with Jesus, the one who had brought such a change in him. Yet Jesus, who only two chapters ago was calling people to follow, tells this man to stay where he is. Why? Perhaps because he can do more good sharing his story with those who knew him before.

Dramatic or not, all of us have a story of how God has changed us. And the people who are likely to be most open to that story are those who know us the best.

PRAYER

Thank you Lord for the ways you change us for the better. Please let those changes be visible in us so that others may see them and give you glory. Amen.

The Power of a Personal Story

Acts 4.1-22

> [The Council] said, "What will we do with them? For it is obvious to all who live in Jerusalem that a notable sign has been done through them; we cannot deny it. But to keep it from spreading further among the people, let us warn them to speak no more to anyone in this name." But Peter and John answered them, "Whether it is right in God's sight to listen to you rather than to God, you must judge; for we cannot keep from speaking about what we have seen and heard." (verses 16-17, 19-20)

Jerusalem was buzzing with a story that hardly seemed credible. Peter and John, two of Jesus' followers, had apparently healed a beggar who could not walk. This man would have been well known, asking people for money as they made their way to the Temple.

The Council of local leaders bring Peter and John in for questioning, but they refuse to be intimidated. When commanded to stop talking about Jesus they respond, "We cannot keep from speaking about what we have seen and heard."

In Acts, which records the activities of the first Christians after Jesus had ascended to heaven, we see that while the preaching of the early Church focuses on the facts of the incarnation, death, and resurrection of Jesus, it also highlights the personal stories of the speakers – "all we have seen and heard."

We all have a personal story of God's presence in our lives. And these stories are powerful.

PRAYER

Thank you God for the story of your presence in my life. Please remind me of the power of that story, that I might give you praise. Amen.

Sharing
Our Story

READING John 4.1-42

> Just then his disciples came. They were astonished that he was speaking with a woman, but no one said, "What do you want?" or, "Why are you speaking with her?" Then the woman left her water jar and went back to the city. She said to the people, "Come and see a man who told me everything I have ever done! He cannot be the Messiah, can he?" Many Samaritans from that city believed in him because of the woman's testimony, "He told me everything I have ever done."
> (verses 27-29, 39)

Hannah Steele writes in *Living His Story*: "Each Saturday *The Guardian* features an article called 'Experience', which focuses on the story of an ordinary individual who has a tale to tell about their life. These stories range from the near miraculous – the man who survived 76 days adrift a raft on the Atlantic Ocean – to the inspiring stories of the amputee who trained to be a professional tap dancer on stage. Some stories make you weep... Others are more humorous... The point is, anyone is free to write in and share their story and we, the reader, are irresistibly drawn by them."

Some Christians fear talking about their faith because they don't think they know enough about it or they wouldn't be able to answer difficult questions. But most of us aren't called to be great theologians or preachers. All we are asked to do is to tell our own story. And those stories draw in those who hear them.

PRAYER

Lord, please help us to be willing and able to tell the story of our lives and your presence in them so that others might be drawn to you. Amen.

Attentive Listening

> Now all the Athenians and the foreigners living there would spend their time in nothing but telling or hearing something new. Then Paul stood in front of the Areopagus and said, "Athenians, I see how extremely religious you are in every way. For as I went through the city and looked carefully at the objects of your worship, I found among them an altar with the inscription, 'To an unknown god.' What therefore you worship as unknown, this I proclaim to you."
> (verses 20-23)

You may have heard the saying, "God gave us two ears and one mouth, so we should listen twice as much as we speak."

When we think about Christians sharing their faith, the image that sometimes comes to mind is of one person – the Christian – doing a lot of talking, often with something that sounds a lot like a prepared presentation, while the other person is expected to listen.

St Paul was a great talker. On one occasion he spoke for so long into the night that a young man sitting in a window dozed off and fell to the ground below. But here we see that he took the time to "listen" to his context as well. That listening then shaped the way he communicated when it was his moment to speak.

We aren't the only ones with stories to share. If we want to be able to speak, about our faith or anything else, we should first take time to listen.

PRAYER

Loving God, every person we meet has a story to share. Help us to take the time to listen, to pay attention, and to be enriched by what we hear. Amen.

Be Prepared

READING **1 Peter 3.13-16** (NLT)

Now, who will want to harm you if you are eager to do good? But even if you suffer for doing what is right, God will reward you for it. So don't worry or be afraid of their threats. Instead, you must worship Christ as Lord of your life. And if someone asks about your hope as a believer, always be ready to explain it. But do this in a gentle and respectful way. Keep your conscience clear. Then if people speak against you, they will be ashamed when they see what a good life you live because you belong to Christ.

As a teenager, I attended a church youth group where on one occasion we were asked to write down our testimony, the story of how we had become Christians and what difference our faith had meant to us. We then shared our testimonies with another person in the group.

You might imagine that this would feel very artificial, but I have always been glad of that experience. It helped me to articulate my own story of God, firstly to myself, and then to someone else, in the hope that I would then be a little more confident to share that story with others when the opportunity arose. And I think I was.

Peter tells us, "If someone asks about your hope as a believer" – about your faith in God, in other words – "always be ready to explain it." So we need to prepare to do this well, and as Peter reminds us, with gentleness and respect.

PRAYER

Gracious God, help us to be prepared to share our own story, the reason we have for putting our hope in you. Please give us those opportunities, and then help us to take them. Amen.

Living

Your Story

READING 1 Thessalonians 2.4-8 (NLT)

For we speak as messengers approved by God to be entrusted with the Good News. Our purpose is to please God, not people. He alone examines the motives of our hearts. Never once did we try to win you with flattery, as you well know. And God is our witness that we were not pretending to be your friends just to get your money! As for human praise, we have never sought it from you or anyone else. As apostles of Christ we certainly had a right to make some demands of you, but instead we were like children among you. Or we were like a mother feeding and caring for her own children. We loved you so much that we shared with you not only God's Good News but our own lives, too.

Ralph Waldo Emerson said, "What you do speaks so loudly that I cannot hear what you are saying."

Hannah Steele writes: "Paul knew that the gospel story could never be communicated purely with words but it had to be lived as well. Our story becomes more authentic to people when they see that it really does impact the way we live our lives. It is often through our daily lives that we demonstrate the topsy-turvy way of the kingdom of God. In a culture where people are more interested in whether things work than whether things are true, our lived experience becomes a potent advocate in our everyday witness."

In other words, people need to see the authenticity of our story in who we are if they are to be truly touched by the story we speak about.

PRAYER

Jesus, please help us to tell the story of your love and goodness through the way we live as well as in the words we say. Amen.

Communicating like Jesus

Christians are called to be witnesses to Christ in their lives and speech. Theologian Stefan Paas says "[Witness] is nothing more than the fostering of natural human relationships, while being unembarrassed about the Christian faith." Good communication is key to witness. We will learn this week from Jesus the master communicator.

ACTION

This week, pay attention to how you communicate with people. What difference does it make to try to apply these communication lessons from Jesus? Write down what you notice in a notebook or journal.

All Sorts
of People

READING Matthew 11.16-19

> Jesus said: "But to what will I
> compare this generation? It is like
> children sitting in the marketplaces
> and calling to one another, 'We played
> the flute for you, and you did not
> dance; we wailed, and you did not
> mourn.' For John came neither eating
> nor drinking, and they say, 'He has a
> demon'; the Son of Man came eating
> and drinking, and they say, 'Look,
> a glutton and a drunkard, a friend
> of tax collectors and sinners!' Yet
> wisdom is vindicated by her deeds."

The letters PLU are sometimes used as
shorthand for the phrase "people like us".
This phrase is meant positively, identifying
someone as a person who will fit in, who

will belong, who we will like. It's a human tendency to gravitate to people like us. It makes life easier when we all see things the same way.

Jesus did not spend his time with people like him. In fact, he was frequently criticised for the people whose company he seemed to enjoy. Tax collectors, prostitutes, beggars, the disabled – in other words, all the people that polite society disdained – were welcomed into his presence.

What about us? Who do we spend our time with? Other church people? People who share our values, or our educational backgrounds, people of the same class or ethnicity? How can we be more like Jesus, and spend our time with other kinds of people?

PRAYER

Lord Jesus, thank you that you spent your time with all kinds of people. Please help us to relate well to people who are different from us, and to learn from them. Amen.

Different People, Different Approach

Mark 5.21-43

> Then one of the leaders of the synagogue named Jairus came and, when he saw him, fell at his feet and begged him repeatedly, "My little daughter is at the point of death. Come and lay your hands on her, so that she may be made well, and live." So he went with him. And a large crowd followed him and pressed in on him. Now there was a woman who had been suffering from haemorrhages for twelve years. She had endured much under many physicians, and had spent all that she had; and she was no better, but rather grew worse. (verses 22-26)

Some of us were taught as children that fairness involves treating everybody the same. On that basis, Jesus doesn't seem to have treated people very fairly. It is striking how his interactions with people vary. Jesus was not like a politician or leader with a small number of set questions or phrases to offer people. ("Have you come far?" "And what do you do?") Rather, every conversation, every interaction was unique.

We see this in this reading that we are looking at over two days. The way Jesus responds to Jairus and the suffering woman are not the same. Jairus is a man in authority, used to giving clear instructions and getting his way. Jesus senses the urgency in his request, stops what he is doing and goes with him. The woman is afraid, ashamed, vulnerable. Jesus senses that too, and deals with her in quite a different way. How can I respond to the people I meet in ways that recognise their uniqueness?

PRAYER

Creator God, thank you that you have made us all different. Help me to appreciate the uniqueness of every person we meet and respond to them accordingly. Amen.

Allowing

Interruptions

READING Mark 5.21-43

[The woman] had heard about Jesus, and came up behind him in the crowd and touched his cloak, for she said, "If I but touch his clothes, I will be made well." Immediately her haemorrhage stopped; and she felt in her body that she was healed of her disease. Immediately aware that power had gone forth from him, Jesus turned about in the crowd and said, "Who touched my clothes?" But the woman, knowing what had happened to her, came in fear and trembling, fell down before him, and told him the whole truth. He said to her, "Daughter, your faith has made you well; go in peace, and be healed of your disease." (verses 27-30, 33-34)

I'm always too busy. Friends have pointed out that when I'm not required to be busy, I add things to my life so that I become busy again. Unfortunately, this means I can be impatient with interruptions. The phone rings, someone wants to speak to me, and inwardly I feel irritated that I am being prevented from getting on with my work. Instead, perhaps, I need to recognise that this conversation is the work that God has for me right now.

We can hardly imagine the tension in Jairus as Jesus, instead of going to his house to heal his daughter as quickly as possible, stops to engage with the suffering woman. But Jesus won't be rushed. Because he will be interrupted, there are two miracles that day instead of one.

PRAYER

Lord, I'm sorry that sometimes I am in too much of a hurry to stop and pay attention to a person you bring before me. Please help me to allow myself to be interrupted by others and by you. Amen.

A Place
of Love

READING **Matthew 9.35-38**

> Jesus went about all the cities and
> villages, teaching in their synagogues,
> and proclaiming the good news of the
> kingdom, and curing every disease
> and every sickness. When he saw
> the crowds, he had compassion for
> them, because they were harassed
> and helpless, like sheep without
> a shepherd. Then he said to his
> disciples, "The harvest is plentiful, but
> the labourers are few; therefore ask
> the Lord of the harvest to send out
> labourers into his harvest."

Hannah Steele writes in *Living His Story*:
"Jesus' starting point with people was from
a place of love. The image of the shepherd
would have been familiar to Matthew's
readers who were steeped in the Old

49

Testament Scriptures and they would have known it as an image used to describe the covenantal relationship between God and his people. The image of the shepherd in the Old Testament is also sometimes used to contrast with the ungodly leaders who are, in effect, *bad* shepherds (Ezekiel 34). Matthew tells us that Jesus is the good shepherd because he has *compassion* on his sheep. The phrase 'had compassion on them' carries a physical connotation, as though Jesus was moved 'in his gut' by the state of the crowds... Jesus is moved by the needs of the crowd but also by the fact that they do not realise who they belong to; they do not know who the shepherd is. They do not know the contentment and peace that comes from knowing that the Lord is their Shepherd."

PRAYER

Thank you Jesus that you are the good shepherd. Help me to know your gentle guidance in my life, and to draw others to be part of the one sheepfold. Amen.

Being
Vulnerable

READING John 4.1-42

A Samaritan woman came to draw water, and Jesus said to her, "Give me a drink." (His disciples had gone to the city to buy food.) The Samaritan woman said to him, "How is it that you, a Jew, ask a drink of me, a woman of Samaria?" (Jews do not share things in common with Samaritans.) Jesus answered her, "If you knew the gift of God, and who it is that is saying to you, 'Give me a drink,' you would have asked him, and he would have given you living water." (verses 7-10)

ooked at part of this passage last week.
look at the beginning of the story.
time, do read the whole thing.

There is a power imbalance in this meeting. Jesus is a man, a Jew, a teacher with followers, a speaker who commands large crowds. His conversation partner is a woman in a patriarchal world, a Samaritan in a society that discriminated against them, a woman who has been married multiple times in a culture where she would be disdained as a result. There is no doubt where the power lies between them.

And yet Jesus makes himself vulnerable by asking this woman for a drink. He begins by acknowledging his thirst, a need that he could not meet but which she could. From that exchange flows the longest conversation with Jesus that we have in the Gospels, a dialogue that changed a life and a community.

PRAYER

Jesus, thank you that you made yourself vulnerable, in your birth, in your death, and in your conversations with others. Please help us to do likewise. Amen.

Good

Questions

READING Mark 10.46-52

> They came to Jericho. As Jesus and
> his disciples and a large crowd were
> leaving Jericho, Bartimaeus son of
> Timaeus, a blind beggar, was sitting
> by the roadside. When he heard that
> it was Jesus of Nazareth, he began to
> shout out and say, "Jesus, Son of David,
> have mercy on me!" Then Jesus said
> to him, "What do you want me to do
> for you?" The blind man said to him,
> "My teacher, let me see again." Jesus
> said to him, "Go; your faith has made
> you well." Immediately he regained
> his sight and followed him on the way.
> (verses 46-47, 51-52)

You would think it was obvious. The man
was blind, and therefore unable to work,
and therefore a beggar. When he called out
to this great healer, "Have mercy on me!",

what might he be asking for, other than the healing of his eyes, so that he might see, be able to work, and feed himself?

Yet Jesus, hearing his voice through the hubbub of the crowd, asks the question. "What do you want me to do for you?" "Let me see", Bartimaeus pleads. And soon, he does.

Sometimes we are too quick to speak, too slow to ask and to listen. When we talk about being a witness, or about sharing our faith (which Christians sometimes call 'evangelism') we can make the mistake of thinking it's all about speaking out the things which we believe to be true. Jesus reminds us that meaningful communication, conversation which leads to change, often begins with a good question, and listening to what is said.

PRAYER

Lord, thank you that you asked good questions, like "What do you want me to do for you?" Help me to ask questions too, and to listen attentively to what is said in return. Amen.

Sharing the Story

When we have really good news, it is natural to want to share it. For example, think about a work colleague who has just become a grandparent for the first time. It can be hard to stop them talking about it! We have a good news story about our own experience of God. This week we will think about how we can share that story with others.

ACTION

This week, look for at least one opportunity to say something about your faith in Christ and what it means to you. For example, when talking about your weekend, you might mention that you went to church and be prepared to say why you go.

God's Story

Our Story

READING Matthew 1.1-17

An account of the genealogy of Jesus
the Messiah, the son of David, the son
of Abraham. Abraham was the father
of Isaac, and Isaac the father of Jacob,
and Jacob the father of Judah and
his brothers, and Judah the father of
Perez and Zerah by Tamar, and Perez
the father of Hezron, and Hezron the
father of Aram, and Aram the father of
Aminadab, and Aminadab the father
of Nahshon, and Nahshon the father of
Salmon, and Salmon the father of Boaz
by Rahab, and Boaz the father of Obed
by Ruth, and Obed the father of Jesse,
and Jesse the father of King David.
(verses 1-6)

I was visiting a central London church for
their evening service, which turned out to
be a service of adult baptism. When the

time came for the Bible reading, someone stood and read the genealogies from the beginning of Matthew's Gospel. At verse 17, the reader stopped and sat down, and I wondered what on earth the preacher was going to make of this passage. The preacher talked us through some of the names in the list, highlighting some of the lesser known characters or those who made terrible mistakes as well as some of the heroes of the faith. After several minutes of this, he turned to those who were to be baptised and said, "Today, your name gets added to this list. Today, your story becomes part of this story of those who have passed through this world in relationship to God. Today, you connect your story with God's story."

PRAYER

Thank you, Lord, that through faith and baptism our stories become part of your story. Help me to share that story in all I do and say. Amen.

Many Tongues

When the day of Pentecost had come, they were all together in one place. And suddenly from heaven there came a sound like the rush of a violent wind, and it filled the entire house where they were sitting. All of them were filled with the Holy Spirit and began to speak in other languages, as the Spirit gave them ability. Now there were devout Jews from every nation under heaven living in Jerusalem. And at this sound the crowd gathered and was bewildered, because each one heard them speaking in the native language of each.

The full name of the book of Acts is "The Acts of the Apostles". But it could also be entitled "The Acts of the Holy Spirit".

Hannah Steele writes in *Living His Story*:

"The work and witness of the Spirit is integral to the book of Acts because the work and witness of the Spirit is integral to Christian mission and evangelism, and indeed the Church. The starting point of Pentecost is an outward explosion in Jerusalem, which ripples throughout the Middle East and eventually even further, fulfilling Jesus' promise that his disciples would be his witnesses in Jerusalem, Judea, Samaria... and even to the ends of the earth (Acts 1.8)."

On the day of Pentecost when Holy Spirit comes, the first thing that happens is that the disciples are enabled to tell the story of Jesus in many languages so that people from all over the world receive the news. The Holy Spirit is always given to help people who haven't heard the story to hear and understand it.

PRAYER

Holy Spirit, please fill us and help us to show the good news of God's kingdom so that others might be drawn closer to God. Amen.

Telling the

Story

Then an angel of the Lord said to Philip, "Get up and go toward the south to the road that goes down from Jerusalem to Gaza." (This is a wilderness road.) So he got up and went. Now there was an Ethiopian eunuch, a court official of the Candace, queen of the Ethiopians, in charge of her entire treasury. He had come to Jerusalem to worship and was returning home; seated in his chariot, he was reading the prophet Isaiah. Then the Spirit said to Philip, "Go over to this chariot and join it." So Philip ran up to it and heard him reading the prophet Isaiah. He asked, "Do you understand what you are reading?" He replied, "How can I, unless someone guides me?" And he invited Philip to get in and sit beside him. (verses 26-31)

Yesterday we saw how the Holy Spirit prompts us to share the story of Jesus in ways that others can understand. Today we see how the same Spirit can give opportunities to share the story that we could not create ourselves. I was once travelling with a group from my church. We were sitting in an airport restaurant on our way home when one of my companions, bolder than me, felt nudged by the Spirit to speak to a man at the next table. I don't know what she said to him, but I saw his eyes open wide and then fill with tears as she spoke to him about Jesus. Whatever she said touched him deeply.

The story we share is both God's and ours. We can feel nervous about speaking about things so profound and personal. But the Spirit helps us in our weakness, if we are open to that guidance.

PRAYER

Lord, thank you for the story I have to tell about the difference you have made in my life. By the Holy Spirit, please give me the words and opportunities to tell that story to others. Amen.

Good News for Everyone

READING Acts 10.1-48

Then Peter began to speak to [Cornelius and his household]: "I truly understand that God shows no partiality, but in every nation anyone who fears him and does what is right is acceptable to him. You know the message he sent to the people of Israel, preaching peace by Jesus Christ—he is Lord of all. That message spread throughout Judea, beginning in Galilee after the baptism that John announced: how God anointed Jesus of Nazareth with the Holy Spirit and with power; how he went about doing good and healing all who were oppressed by the devil, for God was with him. We are witnesses to all that he did both in Judea and in Jerusalem." (verses 34-39)

Prompted by a vision, Peter tells the story of Jesus to a non-Jewish audience. At different times and in different ways, religious people can begin to think of themselves as the "in crowd", those who have been chosen by God for special status in his kingdom, who can therefore look down on others, the "outsiders". Some of our friends who don't call themselves Christians may sadly have experienced this attitude from some who do.

Acts 10 reminds us how misplaced this view is. God's love is for everyone, his purpose is for everyone, and his family is open to everyone. Even when God does call a particular group of people, that calling is for the sake of others, so that God's goodness and glory might be reflected in the world. So we are not Christians just for ourselves, but for others, to bear witness to God's love and longing for everyone.

PRAYER

Loving God, your love is for everyone, and you want every person to know and love you. Help me to be a witness to that love, and a bringer of good news. Amen.

Out There

[Paul] entered the synagogue and for three months spoke out boldly, and argued persuasively about the kingdom of God. When some stubbornly refused to believe and spoke evil of the Way before the congregation, he left them, taking the disciples with him, and argued daily in the lecture hall of Tyrannus. This continued for two years, so that all the residents of Asia, both Jews and Greeks, heard the word of the Lord.

Because telling the story of Jesus and his presence in our lives is such an important and wonderful thing, we can make the mistake of thinking that it should only be undertaken by special people in special places. We have already seen how God can use anybody to share their piece of the story. Today we are reminded that this can happen anywhere. Paul finds that the place of worship and prayer has become a difficult environment for sharing the message, so he moves to another, non-religious, public space.

Many people who do not think of themselves as Christians are reluctant to go into a church building. They don't know what might happen there. They feel they are in somebody else's territory. It can be much easier to share our story with these people in a pub or a living room, on the bus or on WhatsApp.

PRAYER

Please Lord, help me to be aware of your presence in my life all the time, not just in church or when I am praying. And help me always to be willing to share my story with others. Amen.

Never Alone

> Now the eleven disciples went to Galilee, to the mountain to which Jesus had directed them. When they saw him, they worshipped him; but some doubted. And Jesus came and said to them, "All authority in heaven and on earth has been given to me. Go therefore and make disciples of all nations, baptizing them in the name of the Father and of the Son and of the Holy Spirit, and teaching them to obey everything that I have commanded you. And remember, I am with you always, to the end of the age."

Many Christians find the thought of talking to other people about their faith in God quite scary. Today's reading, which comes after the resurrection and just before Jesus ascended to heaven, gives us three encouragements, if we are feeling nervous about this.

First, doubt is no barrier. All of them saw Jesus. Some of them doubted. But Jesus commissioned them all, doubters included.

Second, we do this together. The commissioning is for the whole group, not just certain individuals. Everything is easier and more exciting when do it with others.

Third, Jesus himself is with us. He promises that he will be with us always, when we are conscious of that fact and when we are not.

Anxiety about talking about things that mean a lot to us is understandable, especially if we haven't done it before. But as we share our faith with others, we are never alone.

PRAYER

Thank you, Lord, that you are always with me, and that you don't call me to do anything by myself. Thank you for the presence of your Spirit and the life of the church to which I belong. Amen.

Listening for Echoes

Hannah Steele in *Living His Story* suggests that there are four big questions which every culture must address. These are: 'who are we?'; 'what is wrong?'; 'what's the solution?' and 'what's the future?' By listening for the echoes of those questions in our own culture, and the ways in which culture tries to address them, we can find creative ways to share the story of God which connect with people.

ACTION

This week, think about a book or a film or a TV programme that you have engaged with recently. How does it try to address these four big questions? How would you answer them?

In Athens

(Part One)

READING Acts 17.16-18

> While Paul was waiting for them in
> Athens, he was deeply distressed to
> see that the city was full of idols. So
> he argued in the synagogue with
> the Jews and the devout persons,
> and also in the marketplace every
> day with those who happened to be
> there. Also some Epicurean and Stoic
> philosophers debated with him. Some
> said, "What does this babbler want
> to say?" Others said, "He seems to be
> a proclaimer of foreign divinities."
> (This was because he was telling
> the good news about Jesus and the
> resurrection.)

Hannah Steele writes: "The gospel of Jesus
Christ is the greatest gift we could ever offer
to another person. To share with another

human being the good news that in Christ we are known, loved, forgiven and set free is truly the greatest gift we could give them. But as with other gifts, we need to be thoughtful in how we offer it, giving consideration to what and how we might best connect God's story to the person in view. There is so much we could say about the good news and its themes of love, redemption, reconciliation and God's grace. One of the greatest challenges we face is in knowing where and how to begin the conversation."

Earlier in these reflections we looked briefly at Paul in Athens as an example of attentive listening. Today we see that Paul began his stay looking for cultural clues to help him begin the conversation about Jesus in a way that would connect with the Athenians.

PRAYER

Lord, help us to listen for the echoes and to spot the cultural clues in our own context so that we might share the good news of Jesus in a way that connects with those around us. Amen.

Who Are We?

One of the Pharisees asked Jesus to eat with him, and he went into the Pharisee's house and took his place at the table. And a woman in the city, who was a sinner, having learned that he was eating in the Pharisee's house, brought an alabaster jar of ointment. She stood behind him at his feet, weeping, and began to bathe his feet with her tears and to dry them with her hair. Then she continued kissing his feet and anointing them with the ointment. (verses 36-38.)

The Gospel addresses four deep questions about human experience, and the first is: Who are we?

This story tells us at least three things about this woman, and by implication, about us.

First, she is a sinner. The implication of the story is that she may be a prostitute. But according to Christian tradition we are all sinners, people who get things wrong and fall short. Sometimes, sadly, Christians seem to stop at this point.

Second, though, she is a person of infinite value, made in the image of God, worthy of love and acceptance. She is aware of her own brokenness and capable of repentance and change, as we all are.

And third, she is created for worship, for relationship with God, symbolised in the lavish extravagance of her gesture. And this, too, is true for all of us. It's who we are.

PRAYER

Thank you, God, that you have made us in your image, made us for worship and for love, for relationship with you. Help me to see all people as you see us. Amen.

What's Wrong?

> For the creation waits with eager longing for the revealing of the children of God. We know that the whole creation has been groaning in labour pains until now; and not only the creation, but we ourselves, who have the first fruits of the Spirit, groan inwardly while we wait for adoption, the redemption of our bodies.

C.S. Lewis, in his book *Mere Christianity* writes this: "Enemy-occupied territory—that is what this world is. Christianity is the story of how the rightful king has landed, you might say landed in disguise, and is calling us all to take part in a great campaign of sabotage."

The Gospel story doesn't merely talk about individual human sin and weakness, difficult enough although those things are. It goes on to claim that because of our collective selfishness and distance from God the whole creation has somehow been infected, and fallen under the influence of darkness. This is why our best individual efforts to do better, to be better, tend not to come to very much.

Paul portrays this as a creation which groans like a woman giving birth, longing for freedom, longing for new life. Both Paul and C.S. Lewis would agree that Christians are called to work and pray for that new creation to be born.

PRAYER

Gracious God, I know that things are not the way they should be in the world, or even in me. Please forgive us when we go wrong, and help us to work for your kingdom of justice and peace. Amen.

What's the Solution?

READING John 12.31-33

> Jesus said: "Now is the judgement of this world; now the ruler of this world will be driven out. And I, when I am lifted up from the earth, will draw all people to myself." He said this to indicate the kind of death he was to die.

Yesterday's reflection might have left us slightly despairing about the state of the world we live in, and if it didn't then possibly today's news bulletin will do the job. Thankfully it isn't the end of the story.

The Gospels show how in Jesus God becomes human, entering fully into this world with so much sin and darkness.

Jesus experiences everything that we do – heartache and rejection, hunger and tiredness, as well as love and friendship and joy. The darkness does its worst to him on the cross, and he dies. But because he is God as well as man, death cannot hold him.

In his resurrection, Jesus lights up the darkness and defeats death and sin. It is now possible for each of us, weak and flawed as we are, to know God and God's love for us.

That's good news!

PRAYER

Thank you, God, that in Jesus you came to us, revealing your love and purpose for each of us, dying for us on the cross. Help me to share your love with everyone I meet. Amen.

What's the Future?

> So you see, just as death came into the world through a man, now the resurrection from the dead has begun through another man. Just as everyone dies because we all belong to Adam, everyone who belongs to Christ will be given new life. But there is an order to this resurrection: Christ was raised as the first of the harvest; then all who belong to Christ will be raised when he comes back. After that the end will come, when he will turn the Kingdom over to God the Father, having destroyed every ruler and authority and power.

I write these reflections during the time of the COVID-19 pandemic, when all of us are even more aware than usual of the certainty of death for all of us, and the possibility that our death will come sooner than we expect. Some people have thought that this knowledge renders even the best parts of life futile and meaningless.

Christians have always believed that the resurrection of Jesus means not just that Jesus is raised but that we too will be raised to life after death. In fact, in some sense we are already raised to life if we belong to Christ. So we live our ordinary, temporal life and our resurrected, eternal life both at the same time.

This is a key aspect of the message of Easter, when we get there. And it is good news indeed for all who believe it.

PRAYER

Almighty God, you have offered us the assurance of resurrection to new life. Help us to live in the hope that this bring us, and to share that hope with others. Amen.

In Athens

(Part Two)

READING Acts 17.32-34

When they heard of the resurrection of the dead, some scoffed; but others said, "We will hear you again about this." At that point Paul left them. But some of them joined him and became believers, including Dionysius the Areopagite and a woman named Damaris, and others with them.

Hannah Steele writes: "In Athens, Paul sought to connect the good news of Jesus with the world around him. He engaged in imaginative evangelism. Paul sought to build bridges between people's current experience with his claim that Jesus, the judge of the world, is risen from the dead.

There has never been a more urgent time for us to deploy this kind of creativity and responsiveness in our evangelism since we find ourselves in a culture which has largely forgotten its need of God and in which the Christian narrative holds little or no relevance for people. The world around us is full of 'clues' which point to the gospel story at the heart of the universe. Our task as witnesses is to look for those clues in everyday life and to draw attention to them, arousing curiosity and intrigue in conversations."

PRAYER

Lord, help me to spot the clues which point to the Gospel story and so be able to help the people I know to take steps towards you.
Amen.

Being Found by Jesus

Amazing Grace, a much-loved hymn by reformed slave trader John Newton, says: "I once was lost but now I'm found, Was blind but now I see." Earlier in these reflections we thought about lost things. In this Holy Week we think about some of the different ways in which people are found.

> **ACTION**
>
> This week, commit to praying regularly for five people in your life who do not, as far as you know, have faith in Christ. Look for opportunities to share your story with them.

Long or Short

READING Acts 26.1-32 (NIV)

[Paul said] "What I am saying is true and reasonable. The king is familiar with these things, and I can speak freely to him. I am convinced that none of this has escaped his notice, because it was not done in a corner. King Agrippa, do you believe the prophets? I know you do." Then Agrippa said to Paul, "Do you think that in such a short time you can persuade me to be a Christian?" Paul replied, "Short time or long—I pray to God that not only you but all who are listening to me today may become what I am, except for these chains." (verses 25-29.)

Paul, under arrest, appears before King Agrippa and by way of a defence tells his own story. As he does so, we notice three things.

First is his courage. We sometimes say we need more confidence to talk about our faith. Paul cannot be feeling confident here. Instead he has to reach for courage, as do many of us when our moment to speak comes.

Second is his conviction. He is so convinced of the truth of the Gospel that he wants everyone to become a Christian so that they might know God as he does.

Third is his challenge. He sets a challenge before his listeners to examine for themselves what he has said and to make a response, whether that takes a short time or a long time. And so he reminds us that each person who comes to faith in Christ does so in their own way and at their own speed.

PRAYER

Lord, give me courage to tell my story of faith in you, and patience to allow others to respond in their own way and at their own speed. Amen.

The Road to Damascus

READING Acts 26.12-16 (NIV)

"On one of these journeys I was going
to Damascus with the authority and
commission of the chief priests. About
noon, King [Agrippa], as I was on
the road, I saw a light from heaven,
brighter than the sun, blazing around
me and my companions. We all fell to
the ground, and I heard a voice saying
to me in Aramaic, 'Saul, Saul, why do
you persecute me? It is hard for you to
kick against the goads.' Then I asked,
'Who are you, Lord?' 'I am Jesus, whom
you are persecuting,' the Lord replied.
'Now get up and stand on your feet. I
have appeared to you to appoint you as
a servant and as a witness of what you
have seen and will see of me."

Today we look at some words from earlier in
Paul's defence before King Agrippa, in which

he tells his story of meeting Christ on the road to Damascus. This is such an important story in Paul's life and ministry that the New Testament records it in several different places. Perhaps the only thing that almost everybody knows about Paul is the drama of his conversion. We even talk of someone having a 'Damascus road conversion' when they change their minds about something completely in a moment. It's a powerful and moving story.

It may be that your story of coming to faith has one or more dramatic moments too, and you can identify to some extent with Paul's experience. But that isn't true for many of us. And the assumption that this is what becoming a Christian is supposed to look like can be unhelpful when we evaluate the much more gradual journey that many of us have been on.

PRAYER

Gracious God, thank you for the ways you have brought us to faith in you, whether dramatic or gradual. Please help us to walk alongside others who are on that same journey of faith. Amen.

The Road to Emmaus

READING Luke 24.13-35

> As they came near the village to which they were going, he walked ahead as if he were going on. But they urged him strongly, saying, "Stay with us, because it is almost evening and the day is now nearly over." So he went in to stay with them. When he was at the table with them, he took bread, blessed and broke it, and gave it to them. Then their eyes were opened, and they recognised him; and he vanished from their sight. (verses 28-31)

It's the day of the resurrection of Jesus and two disciples are walking to a village called Emmaus. They are talking about this wild rumour that they have heard, that Jesus is alive, and trying to make sense of it. The risen Christ walks with them, unrecognised, and joins the conversation. Later, he assumes the role of the host at the table, and breaks bread, and in that moment, they recognise him.

For many people, coming to faith is more like the Emmaus Road than the Damascus Road. Jesus is recognised as one who has been there all along, opening the Scriptures, breaking the bread.

Neither one of these is better than the other. Our prayer is that people should come to know the Risen Christ and his presence in their lives. Whether that happens suddenly or slowly matters not at all.

PRAYER

Thank you, Jesus, that you walk with each one of us, that you teach us, that you reveal yourself to us in the breaking of the bread. Help me to recognise you wherever I may find you. Amen.

Proclamation

READING 1 Corinthians 1.21-25

For since, in the wisdom of God, the world did not know God through wisdom, God decided, through the foolishness of our proclamation, to save those who believe. For Jews demand signs and Greeks desire wisdom, but we proclaim Christ crucified, a stumbling block to Jews and foolishness to Gentiles, but to those who are the called, both Jews and Greeks, Christ the power of God and the wisdom of God. For God's foolishness is wiser than human wisdom, and God's weakness is stronger than human strength.

In 1984 the renowned evangelist Billy Graham came to England and preached at sports stadia around the country for a week at a time. I was 18 years old. As a very keen young Christian I hired a coach every night to take people from my school to the nearest event, 50 miles away. One of my school friends recently posted on Facebook the letter that I wrote to him inviting him to come with me, which he did. I was moved that he still had this, 36 years later.

The fact that most people come to faith gradually does not mean that there is no place for this proclamation style of evangelistic preaching. For many, that can be one piece of the puzzle, even if coming to faith is a slow process. And all of us have a part to play. I can't preach like Billy Graham. But I can pray, I can witness to what I have experienced, and I can invite.

PRAYER

Lord, thank you for those who are gifted to proclaim the message of the Gospel. Please bless and use them. And help me to play my part, as I pray and witness and invite. Amen.

Witness

READING Acts 1.7-9

> [Jesus] replied, "It is not for you to know the times or periods that the Father has set by his own authority. But you will receive power when the Holy Spirit has come upon you; and you will be my witnesses in Jerusalem, in all Judea and Samaria, and to the ends of the earth." When he had said this, as they were watching, he was lifted up, and a cloud took him out of their sight.

Hannah Steele writes:

"Our role as witnesses is often more akin to nudging people along the pathway than to running and completing a sprint. Such nudging evangelism requires patience, perseverance and all the creative skills at our disposal. We may meet someone who has barely started along their faith journey and our role is to spark interest in the Christian faith. We may meet someone who has been thinking about the Christian faith for a while and our role might be to patiently and seriously help them work through some of the questions that they have. Thinking in terms of steps along a pathway can free us from the burden of feeling we have to bring someone to a moment of commitment straight away. It can be more helpful to ask the question 'What is the next step this person needs to make on their faith journey?' [and how can I help?]. [This is] beautiful evangelism in practice, responding intelligently and individually to the person before us."

PRAYER

Thank you, Lord Jesus, that you call me to witness to what I have experienced in my faith life, and so bring glory to you. Through the Holy Spirit, please help me to be a good witness to your love. Amen.

The Pearl of Great Price

READING Matthew 13.44-46 (NLT)

Jesus said: "The Kingdom of Heaven is like a treasure that a man discovered hidden in a field. In his excitement, he hid it again and sold everything he owned to get enough money to buy the field.

"Again, the Kingdom of Heaven is like a merchant on the lookout for choice pearls. When he discovered a pearl of great value, he sold everything he owned and bought it!"

What is the most valuable thing you possess? And what did you have to give up to obtain it? Or what would you be willing to lose in order to keep it?

We might answer this in purely financial

terms. My most valuable possession is my home and I give up half my salary every month to keep it.

Or we might think in terms of sentimental value. My mother's engagement ring is the most precious thing I own. It's only mine because she is no longer with us, and I wouldn't give it up for anything.

Or we might think in relational terms. My children are the most important thing in my life, and I have sacrificed greatly for them.

Jesus says that God's kingdom is like that. Some of us who have been Christians for a long time can forget how precious it is to know ourselves loved by God, and so we miss out on the joy of sharing that gift with others.

PRAYER

Loving God, your Son Jesus Christ gave up everything for us. Help us to be truly grateful, and to share the gift of your good news with others so that they might receive it, too. Amen.

"I Have Seen the Lord!"

READING John 20.1-29

But Mary stood weeping outside the tomb. As she wept, she bent over to look into the tomb; and she saw two angels in white, sitting where the body of Jesus had been lying, one at the head and the other at the feet. They said to her, "Woman, why are you weeping?" She said to them, "They have taken away my Lord, and I do not know where they have laid him." When she had said this, she turned around and saw Jesus standing there, but she did not know that it was Jesus. Jesus said to her, "Woman, why are you weeping? Whom are you looking for?" Supposing him to be the gardener, she said to him, "Sir, if you have carried

> him away, tell me where you have laid him, and I will take him away." Jesus said to her, "Mary!" She turned and said to him in Hebrew, "Rabbouni!" (which means Teacher). Jesus said to her, "Do not hold on to me, because I have not yet ascended to the Father. But go to my brothers and say to them, 'I am ascending to my Father and your Father, to my God and your God.'" Mary Magdalene went and announced to the disciples, "I have seen the Lord"; and she told them that he had said these things to her. (verses 11-18.)

Hannah Steele writes in *Living His Story*:

"The story of the gospel of Jesus Christ is the most remarkable we will ever hear. It is a story of redemption, sacrifice and love with the power to transform lives... As we prepare for the celebration of Easter we remember a cosmic turning point in human history when death is defeated and new life is made possible in Christ.

"On that first Easter morning, God could have chosen to make the news of Jesus's miraculous resurrection known in any number of ways. He could have emblazoned a declaration across the sky so all could have seen it and not doubted its veracity. He could have had Jesus appear alive in the presence of the crowd who had bayed for his death. However, God chose the lips of ordinary women, whose hearts were broken with grief, now erupting with joy, to be the vessels through which he would pass on this life changing news. God chose ordinary people with personal stories of redemption and imperfect words, to tell the greatest news there has ever been.

"God continues to use people like you and me to share the life changing news of the gospel of Jesus. We are the ordinary people through whom God is bringing about a revolution of his extraordinary love. The mandate remains the same but the context is different. There is no guarantee that our experience of witness will be easy; we should certainly not underestimate the challenges which lie before us. Our task is that of engaging in evangelism that is both beautiful and imaginative. We are to bear witness in a way that speaks to people's heart and minds, connecting their stories with God's great story so that in Christ they might find new life and meaning. Let us hear his voice this Holy Week calling to us as it did to Mary that first Easter morning; Go and tell. As we seek to live the story of the Gospel we are privileged to reveal his extraordinary love in ordinary ways, putting our name to his story and inviting others to join us as we do so. There is no task more urgent or wonderful than this."

PRAYER

Thank you, loving God, for raising your Son Jesus Christ to life again. Thank you for the difference his resurrection makes to my life and to your whole creation. Please help me today and every day to share this astonishing news through my life and through my words. Amen.

Next Steps

We hope you have enjoyed this #LiveLent journey. Here are some ways you might want to travel further in the faith in the days and months ahead:

Explore God in everyday life with *Everyday Faith*

Everyday Faith provides resources for individuals and churches to help them find and follow God in everyday life – including prayers, reflections and stories. Visit **churchofengland.org/everydayfaith** to find out more.

Take part in *Thy Kingdom Come*

Thy Kingdom Come is a global prayer movement inviting Christians to pray during the nine days between Ascension and Pentecost for more people to come to know Jesus Christ. Find out more about ways you can participate, inspiring stories and further resources at **thykingdomcome.global**.

Sign up for future Church of England reflections

Visit **churchofengland.org** to sign up for future campaigns and resources – including Lent and Christmas reflections. It's free to sign up for emails and you can easily opt out at any time.